Cowboy Malbuch
Die Rodeo Edition mit Pferden

Coloring Pages for Kids

Coloring Pages for Kids
An imprint of Ciparum LLC

Cowboy Malbuch Die Rodeo Edition mit Pferden
© 2017 Ciparum LLC
All rights reserved.
ISBN-10:1-63589-334-8
ISBN-13:978-1-63589-334-2

Coloring Pages for Kids

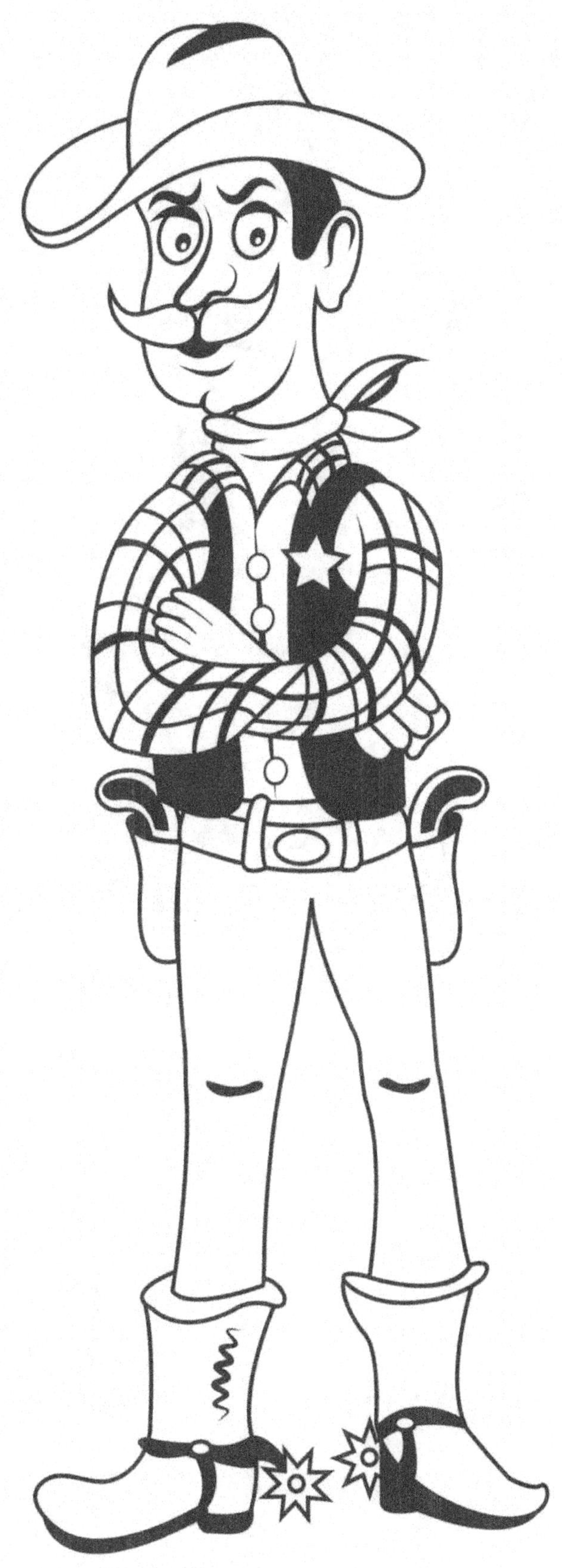

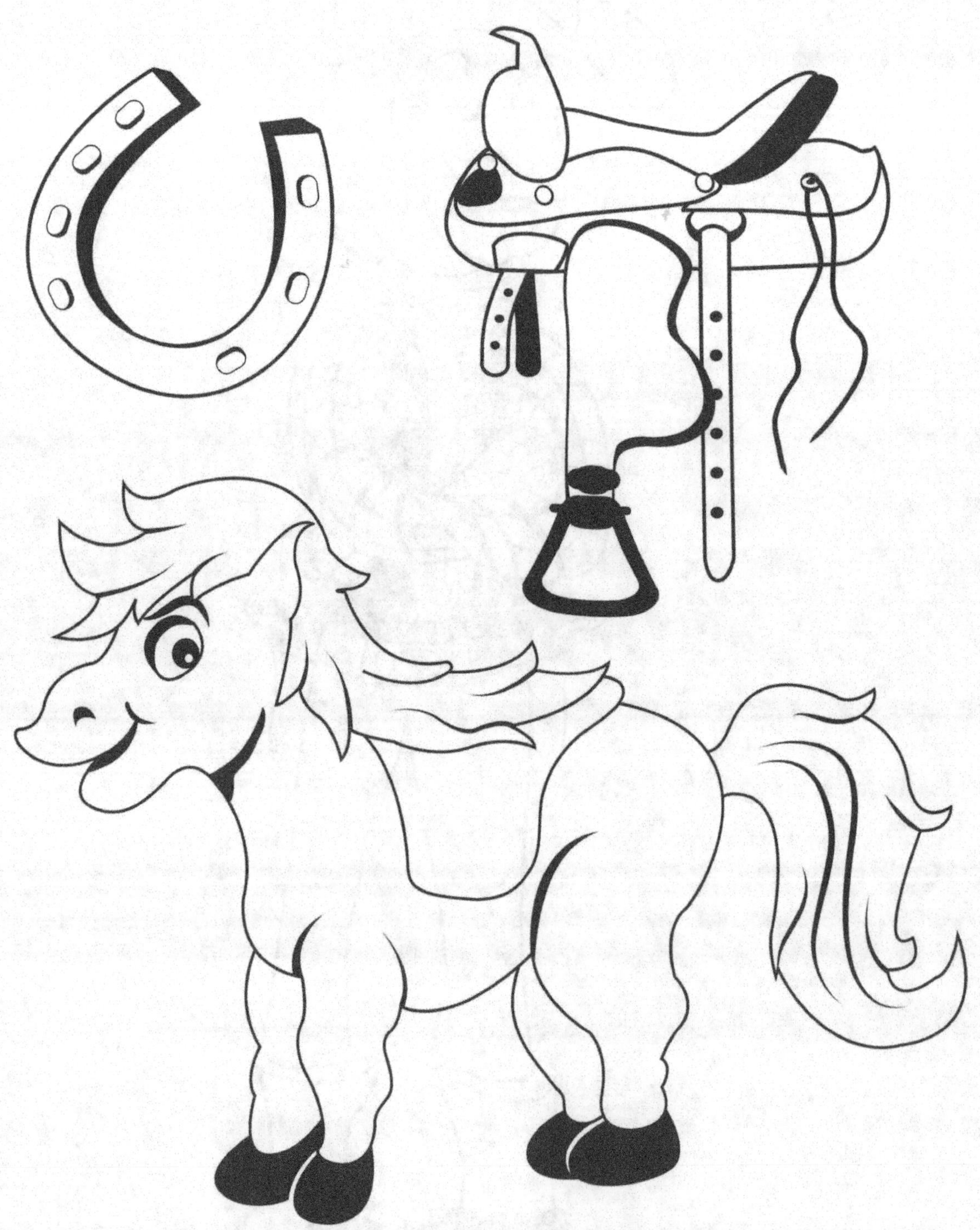

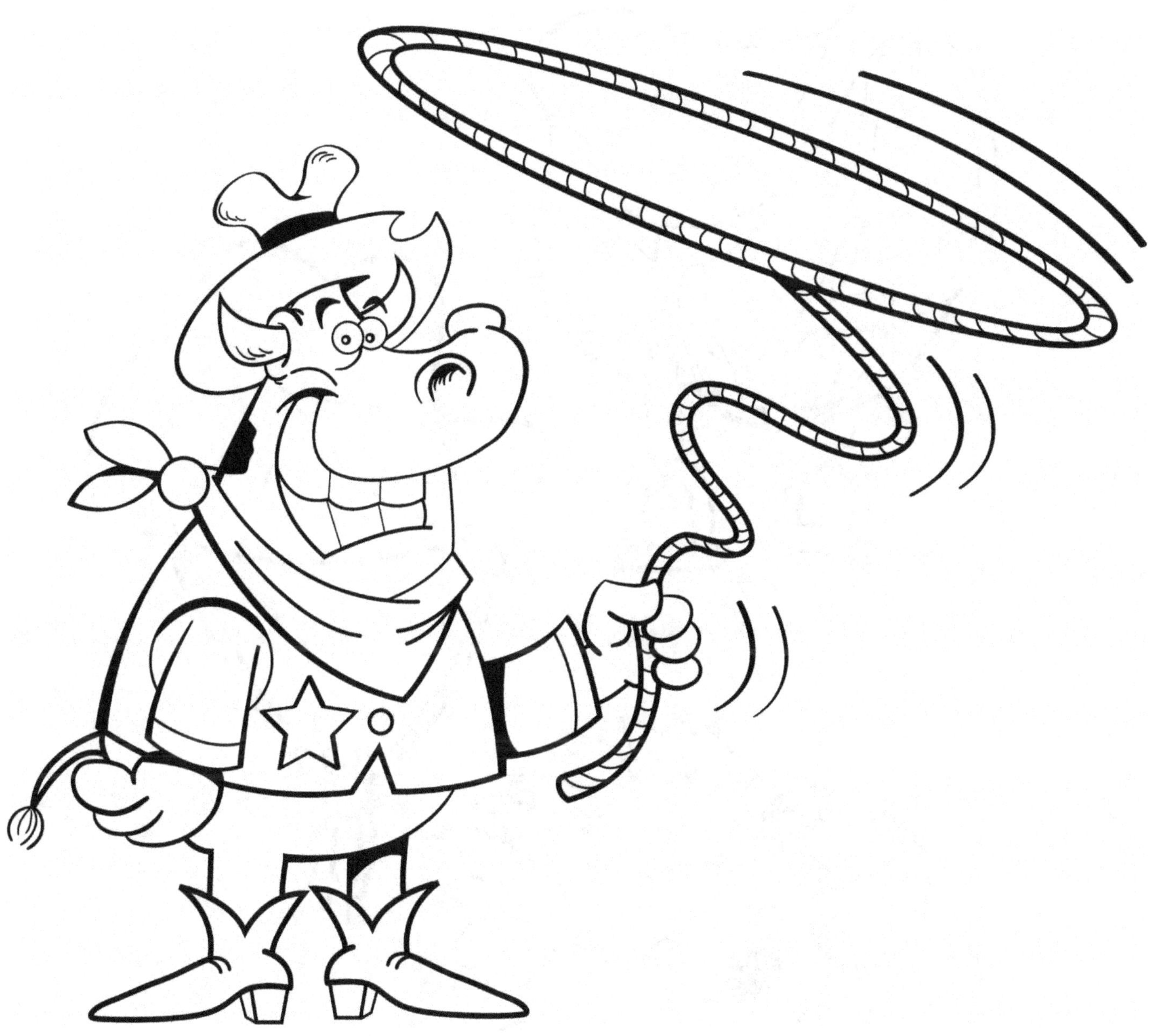

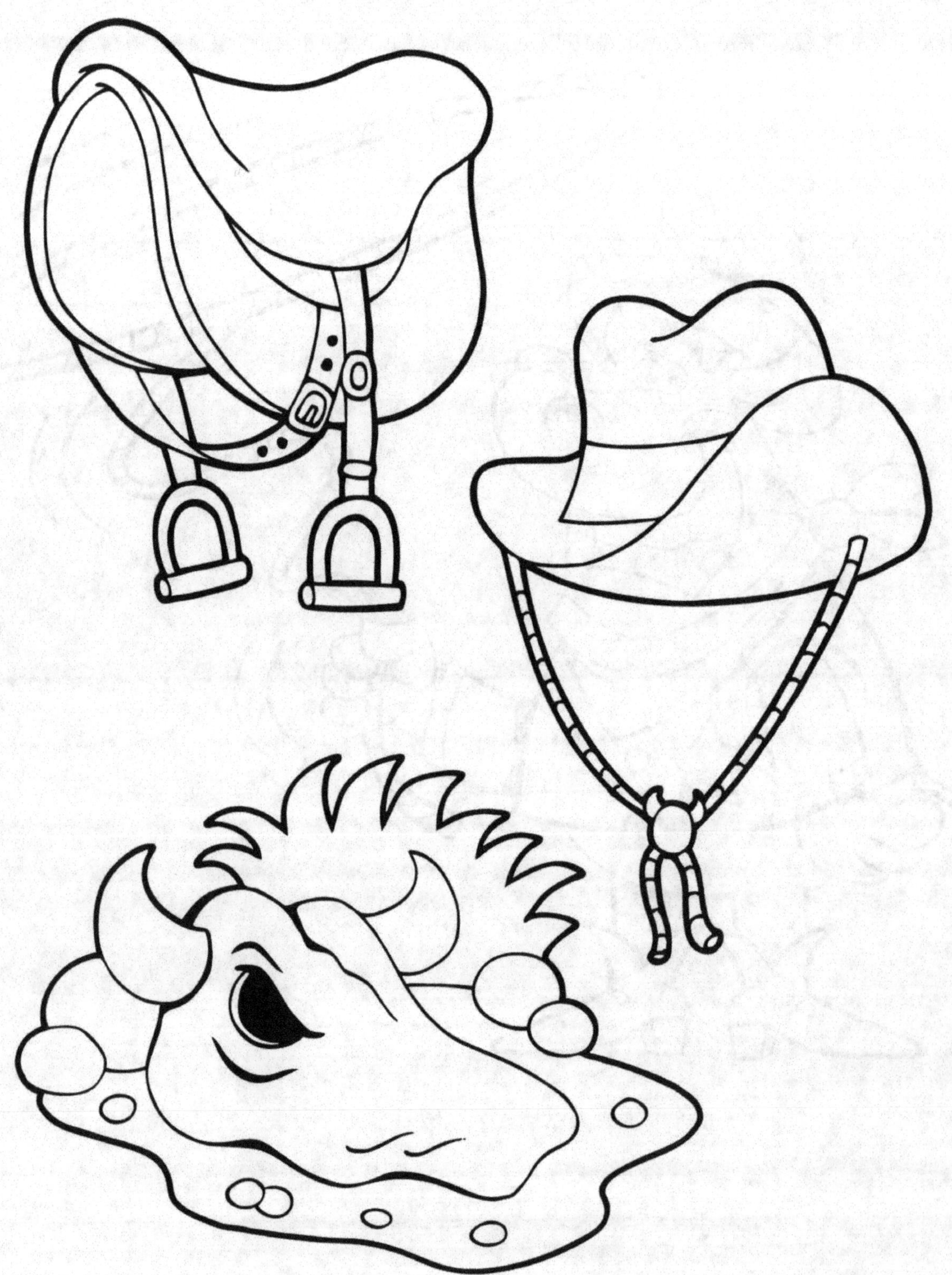

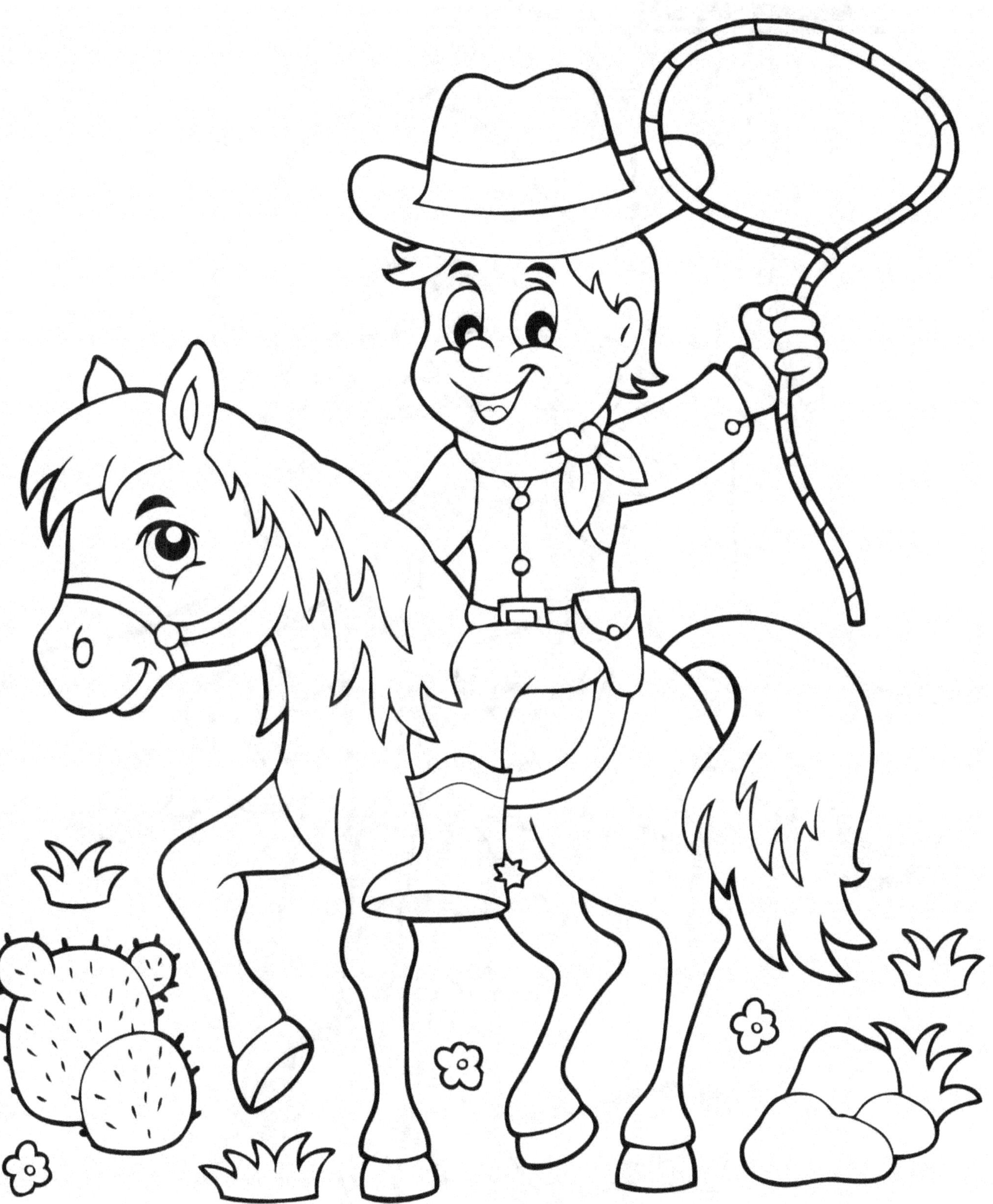

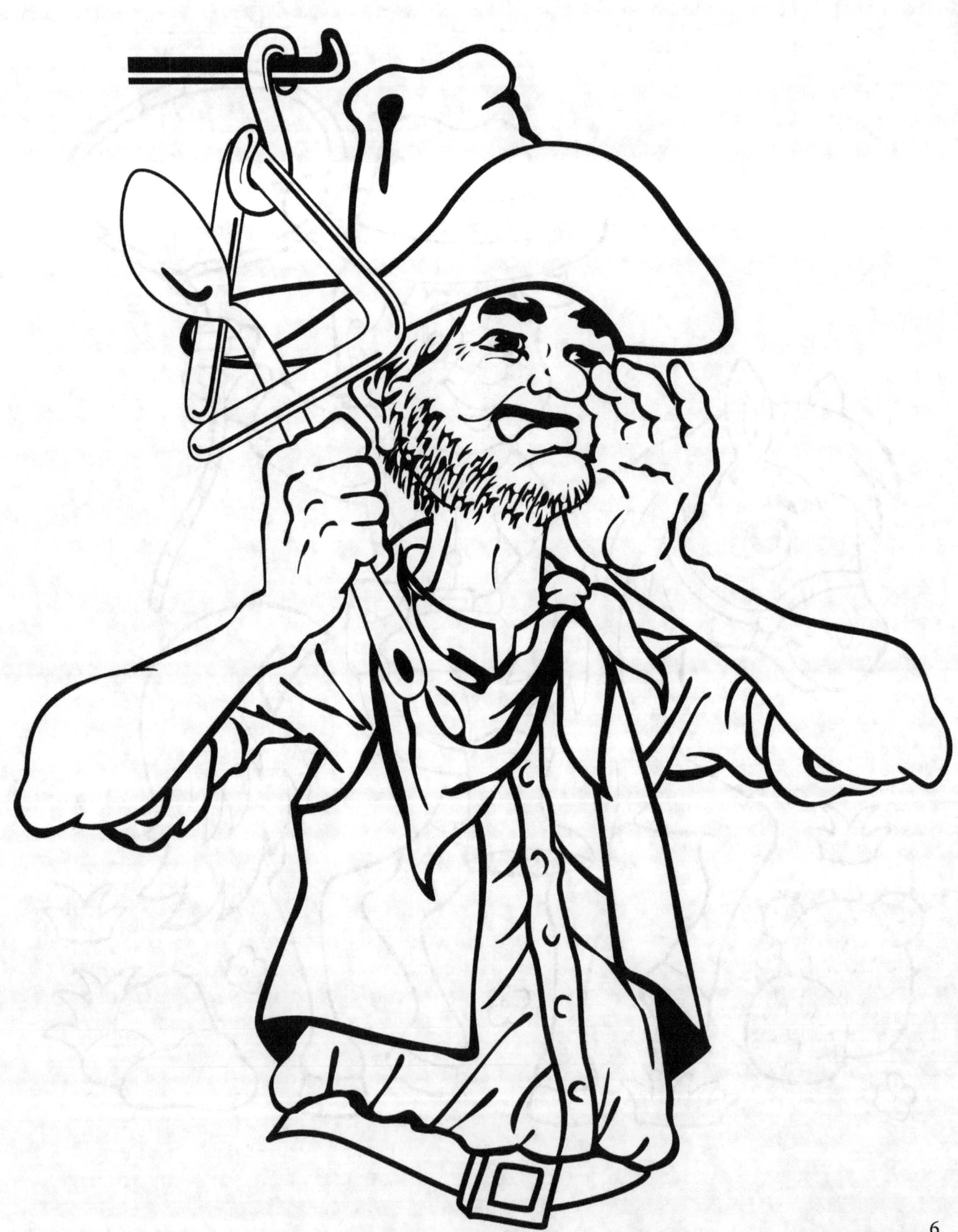

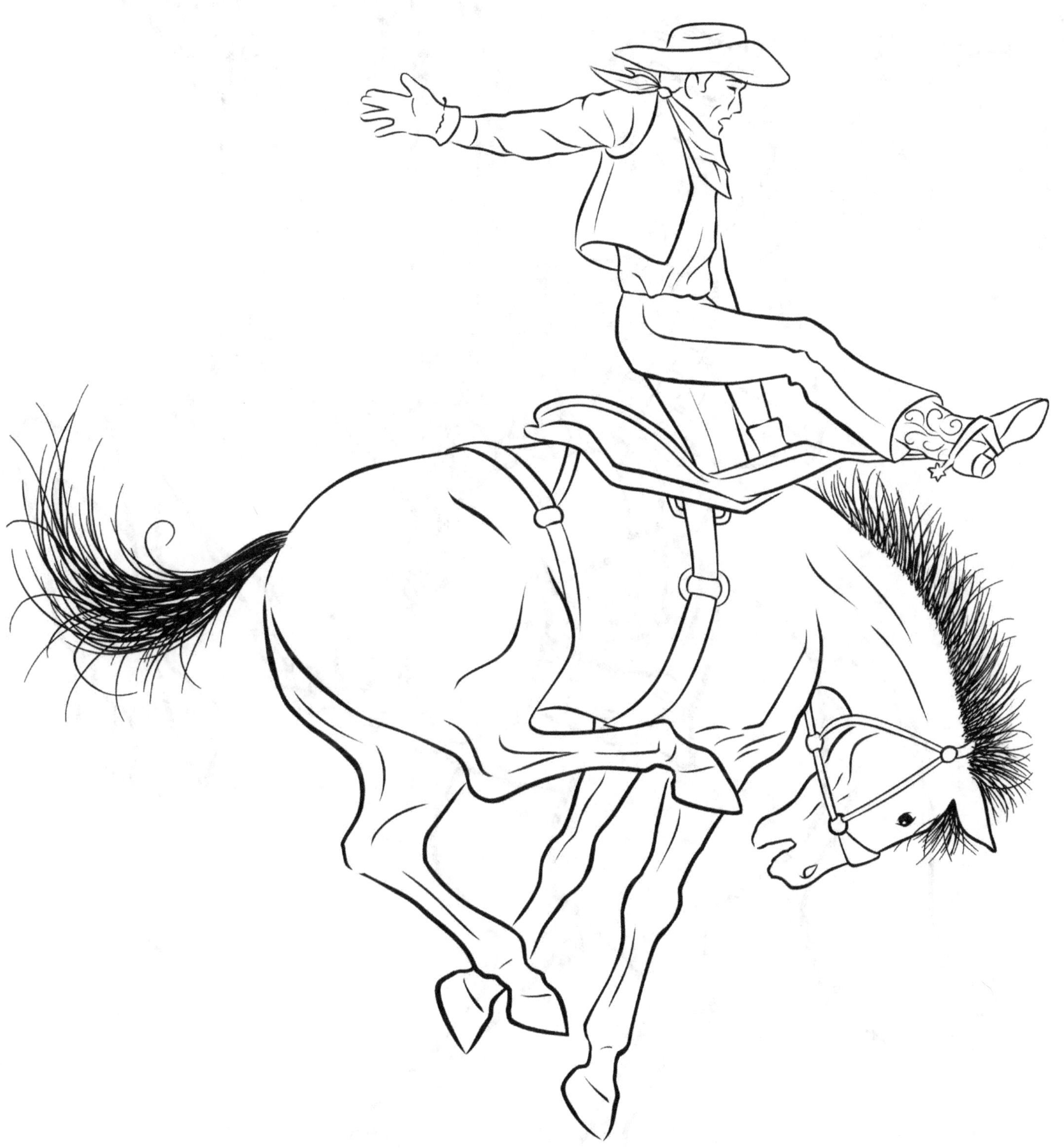

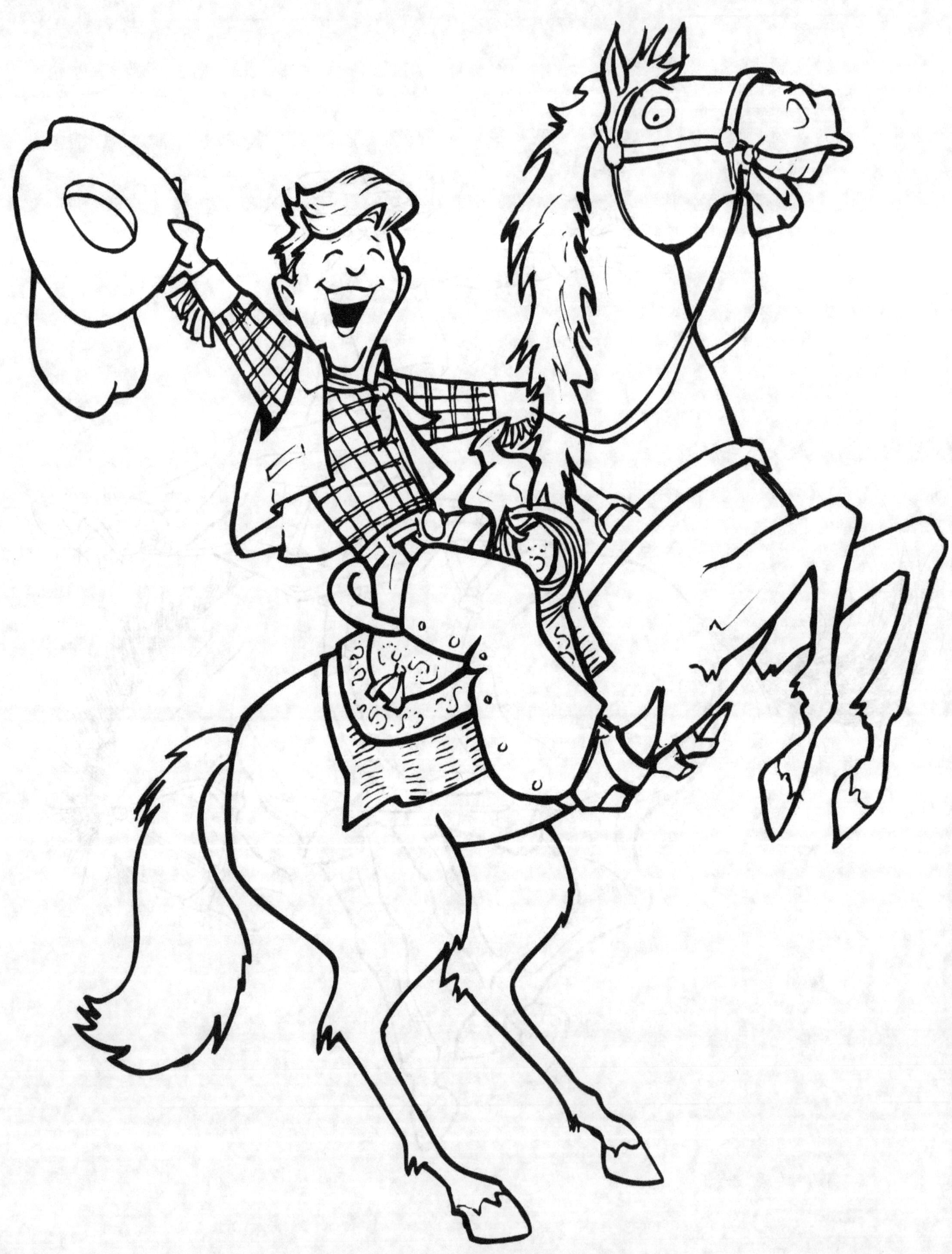

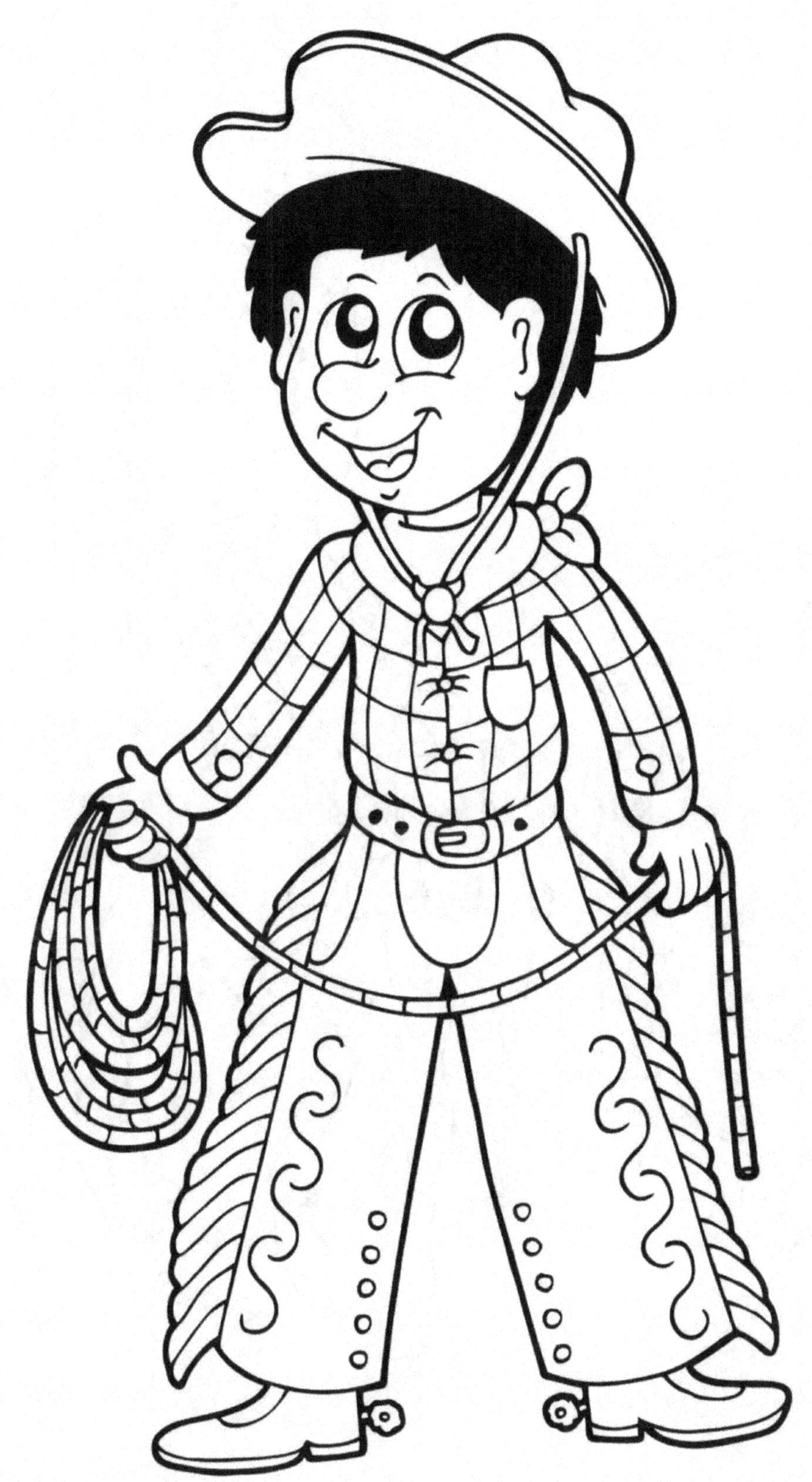

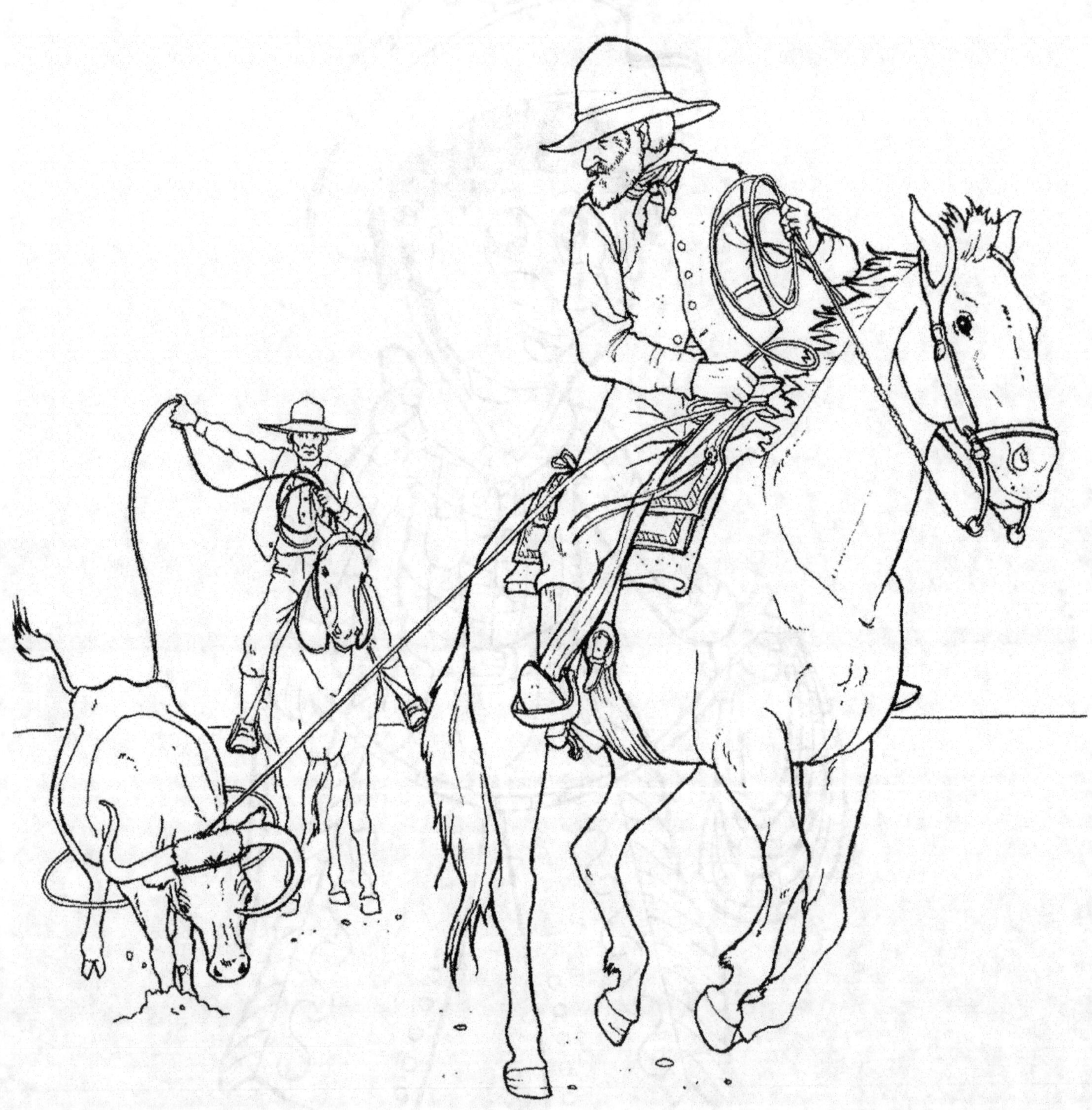

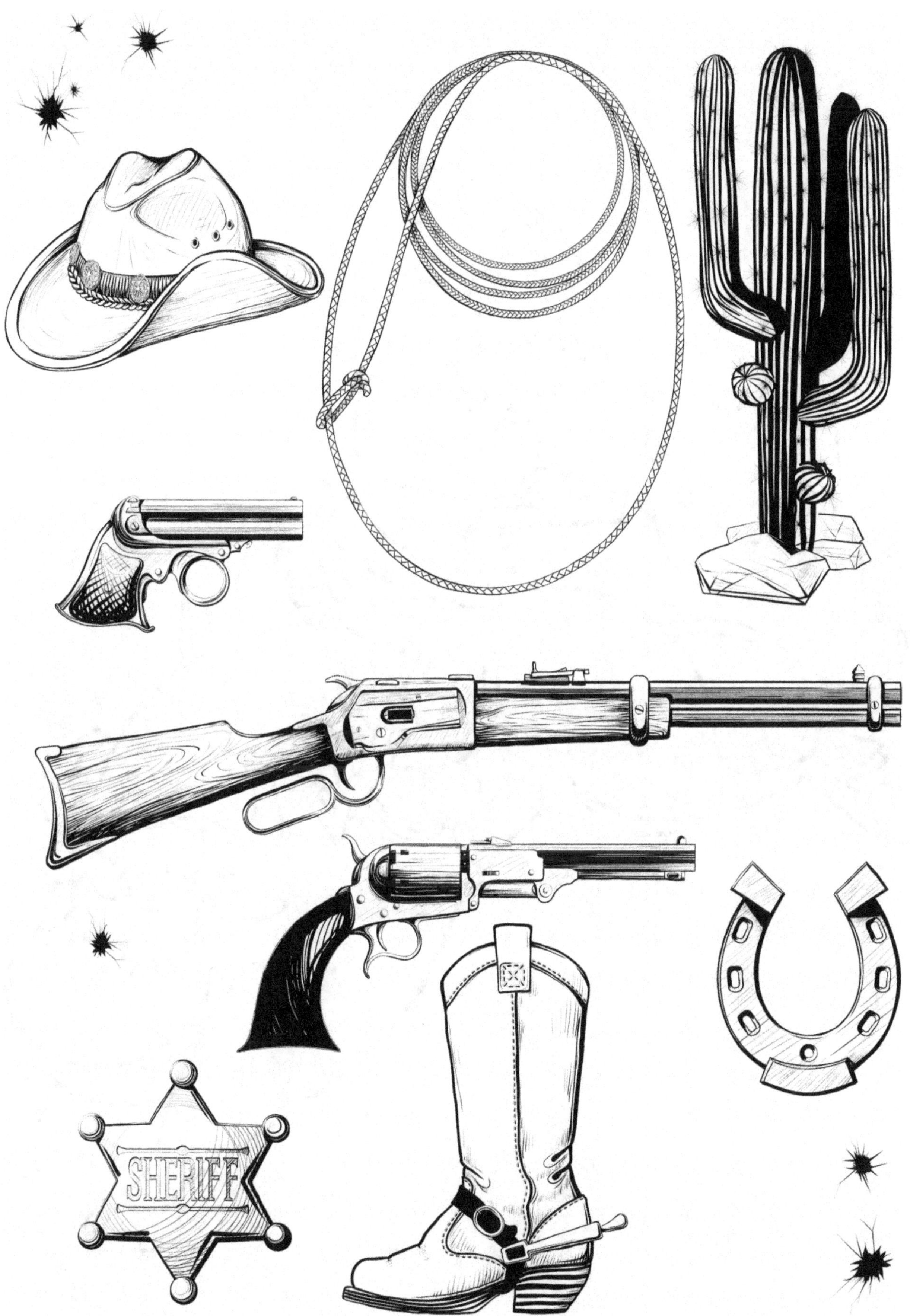

SHERIFF

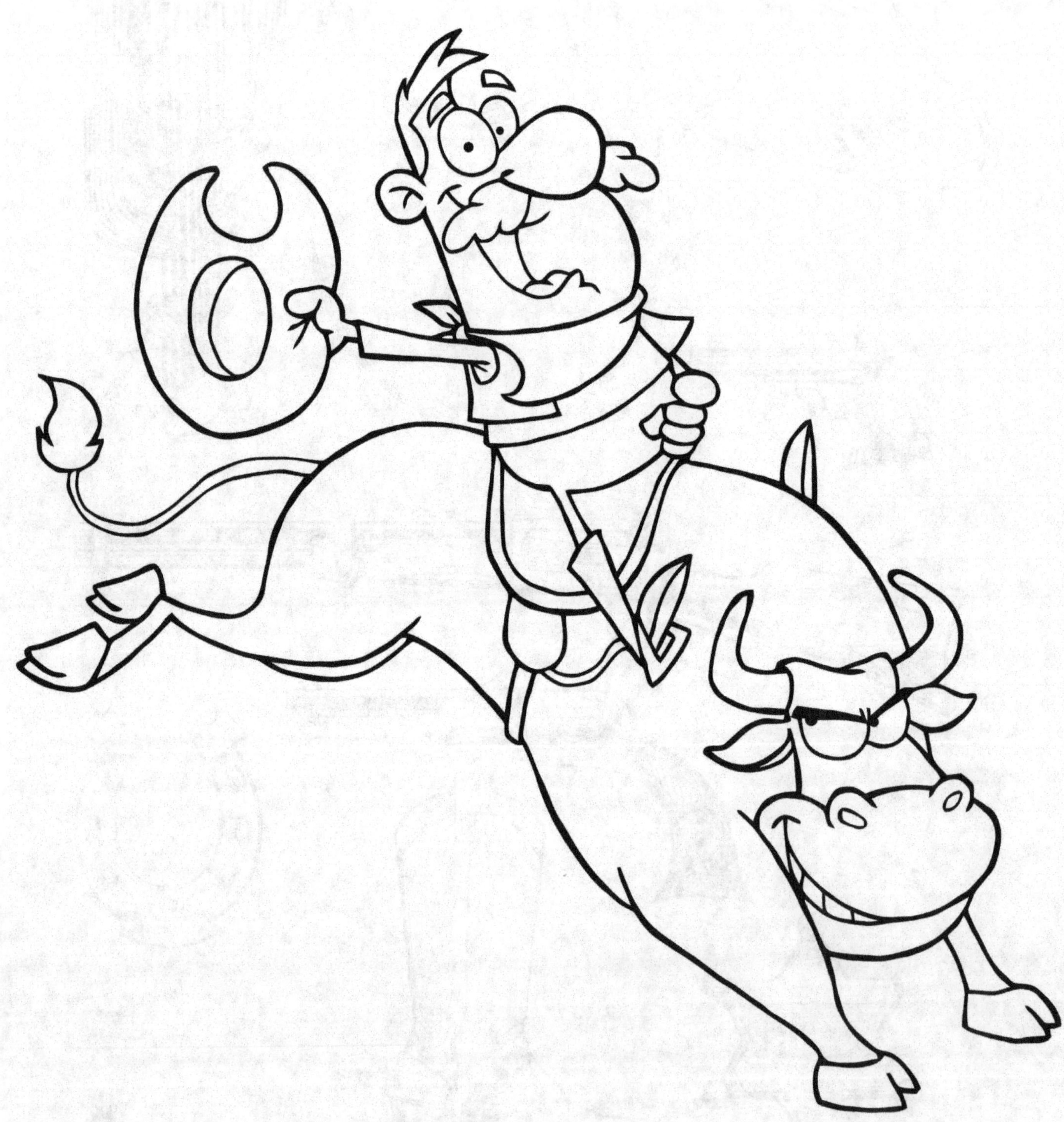

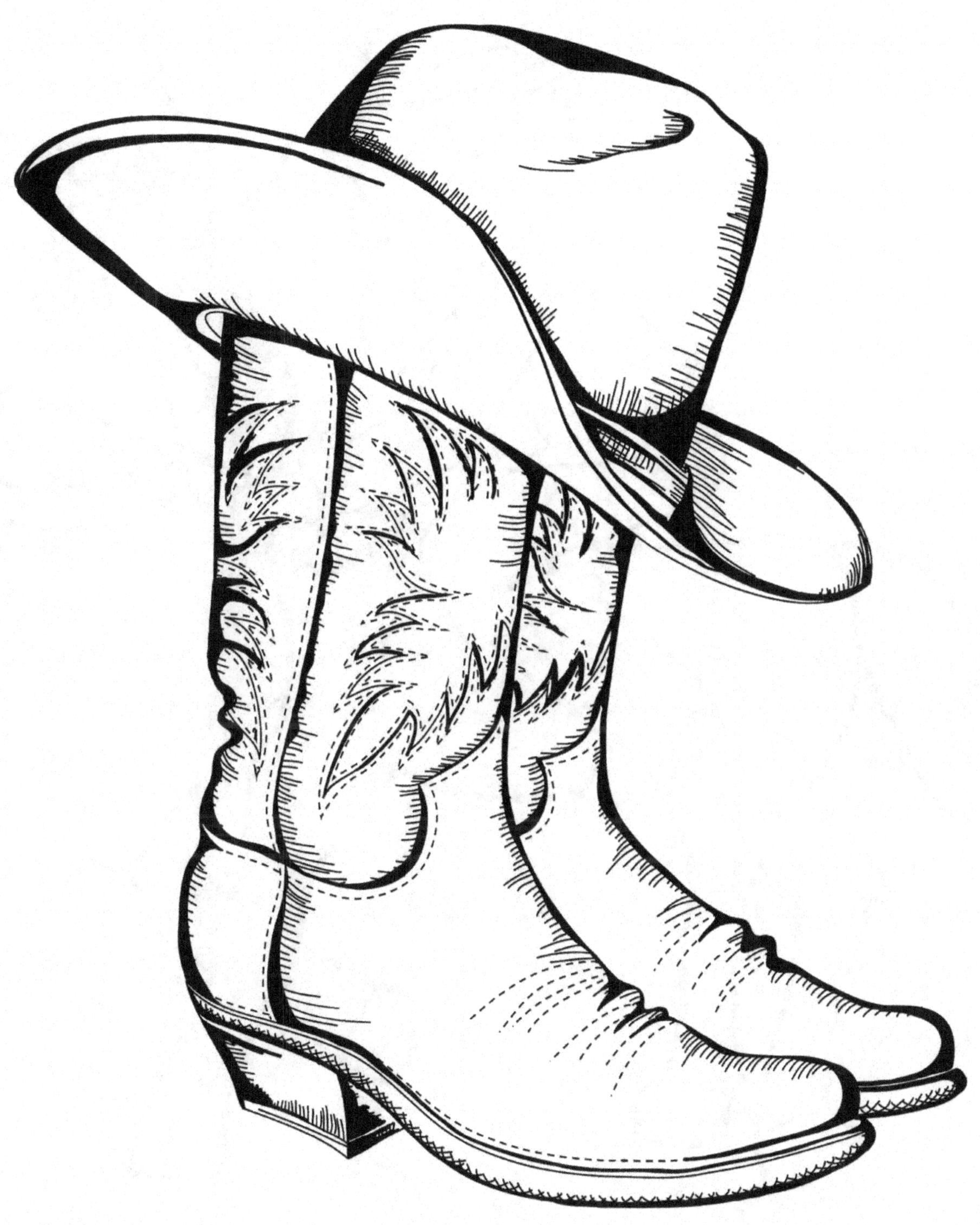

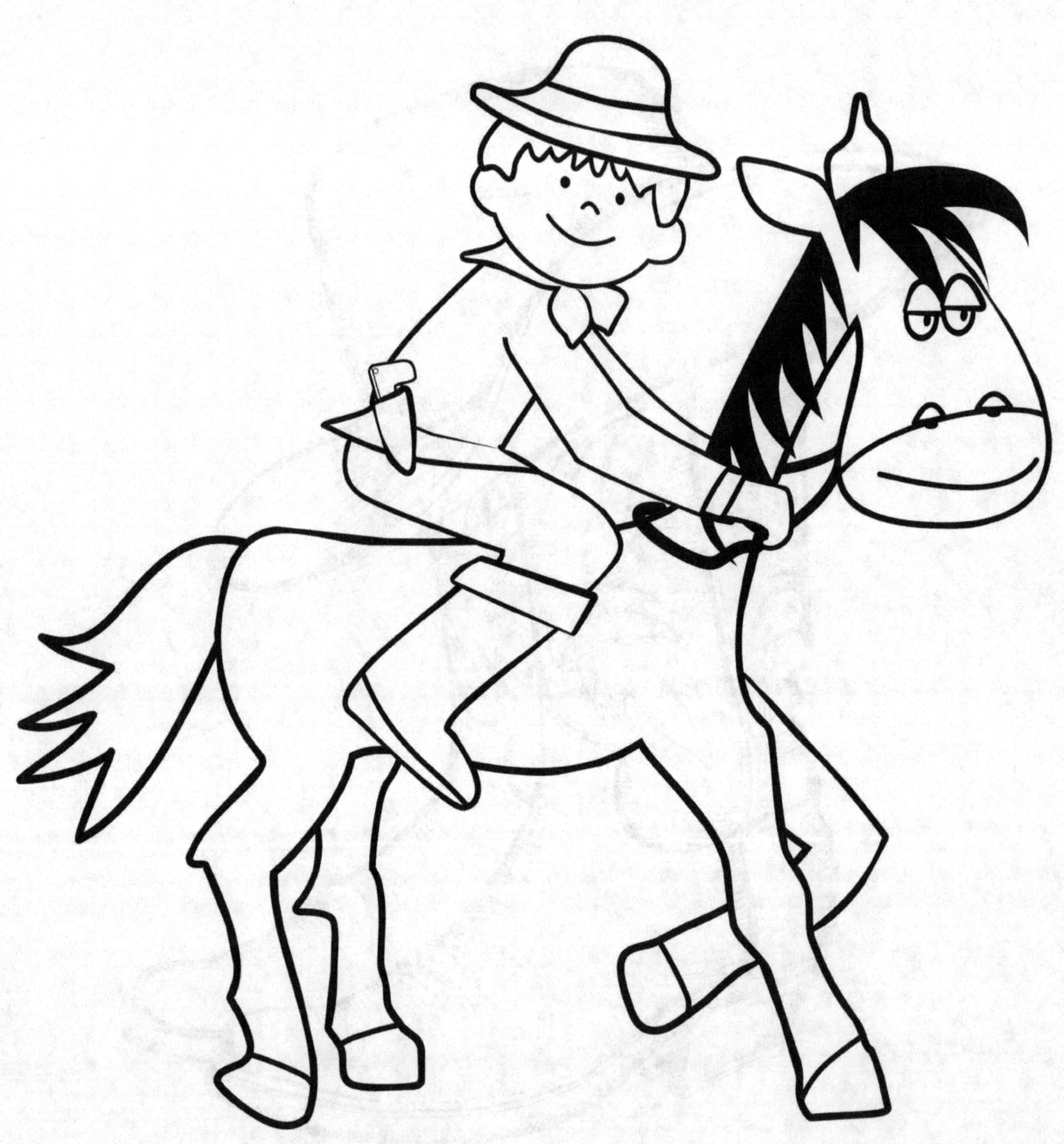

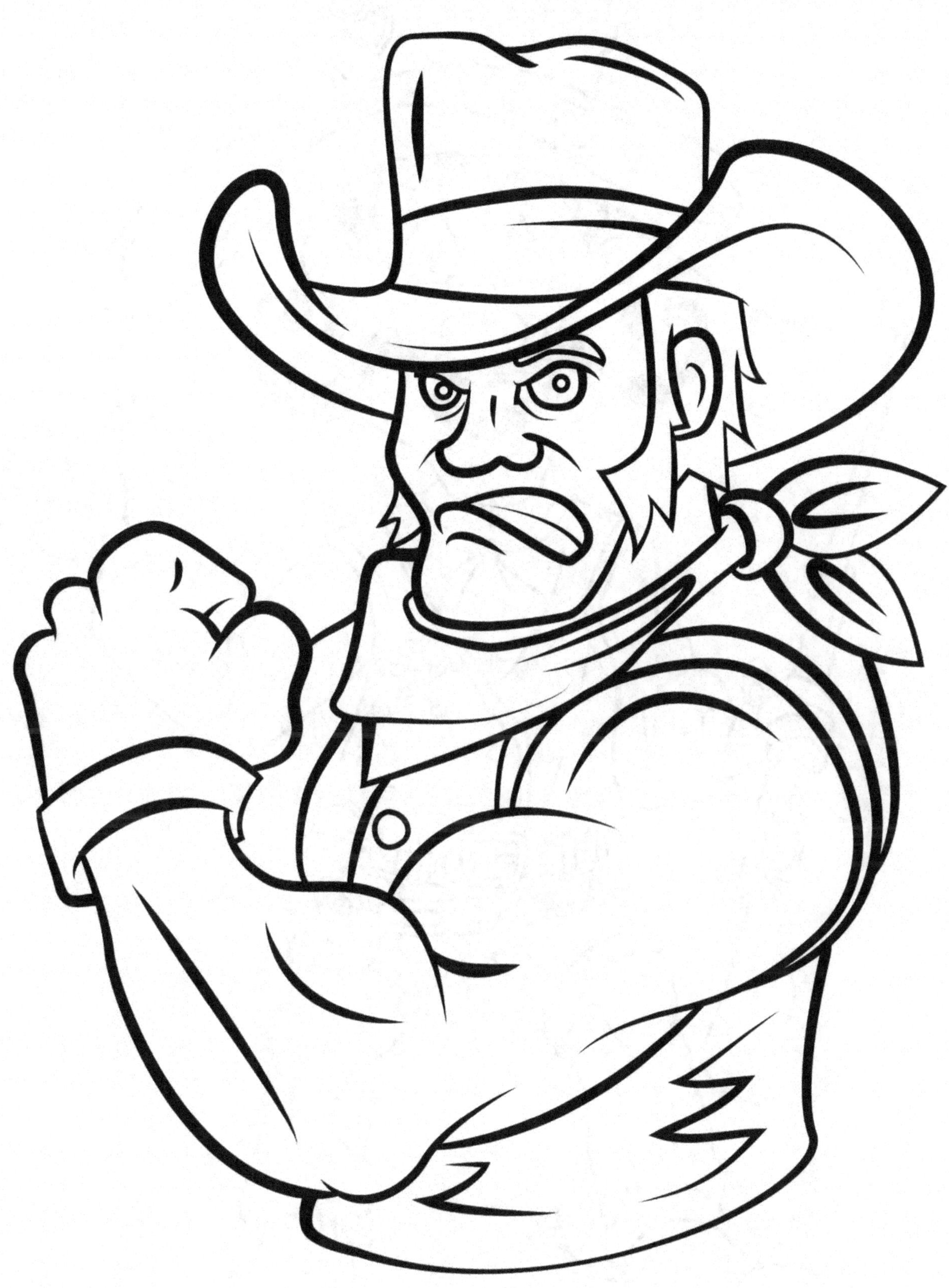

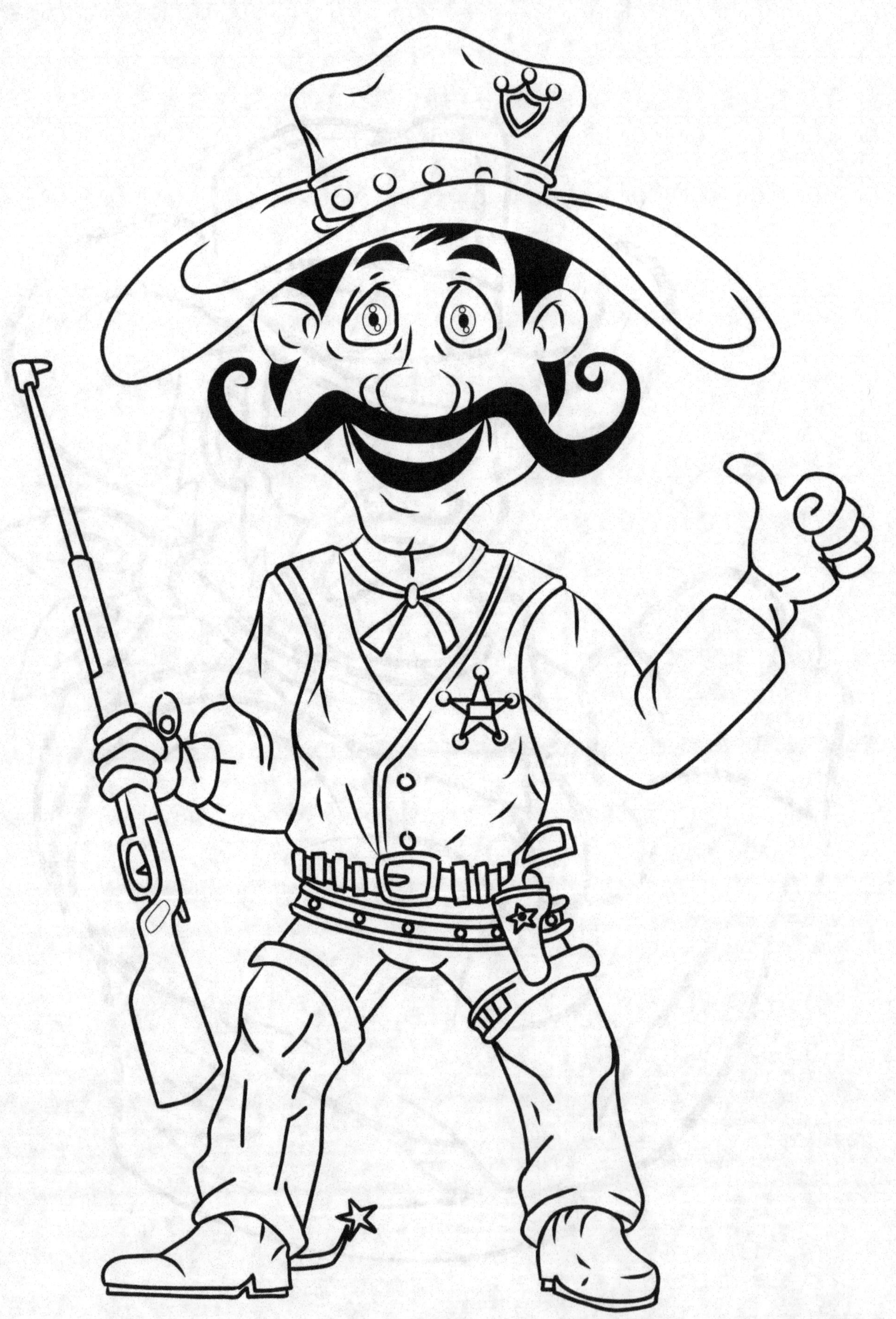

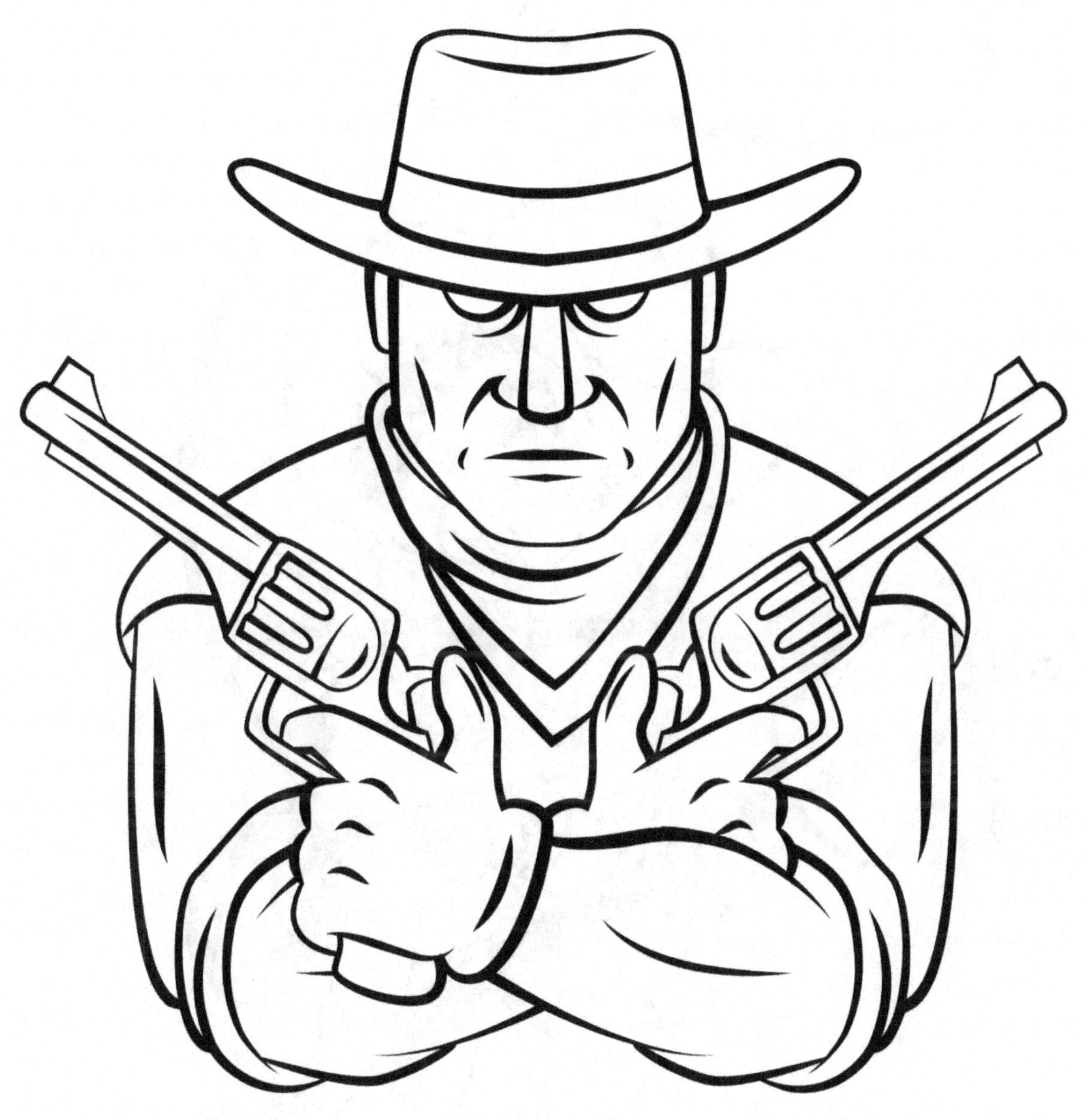

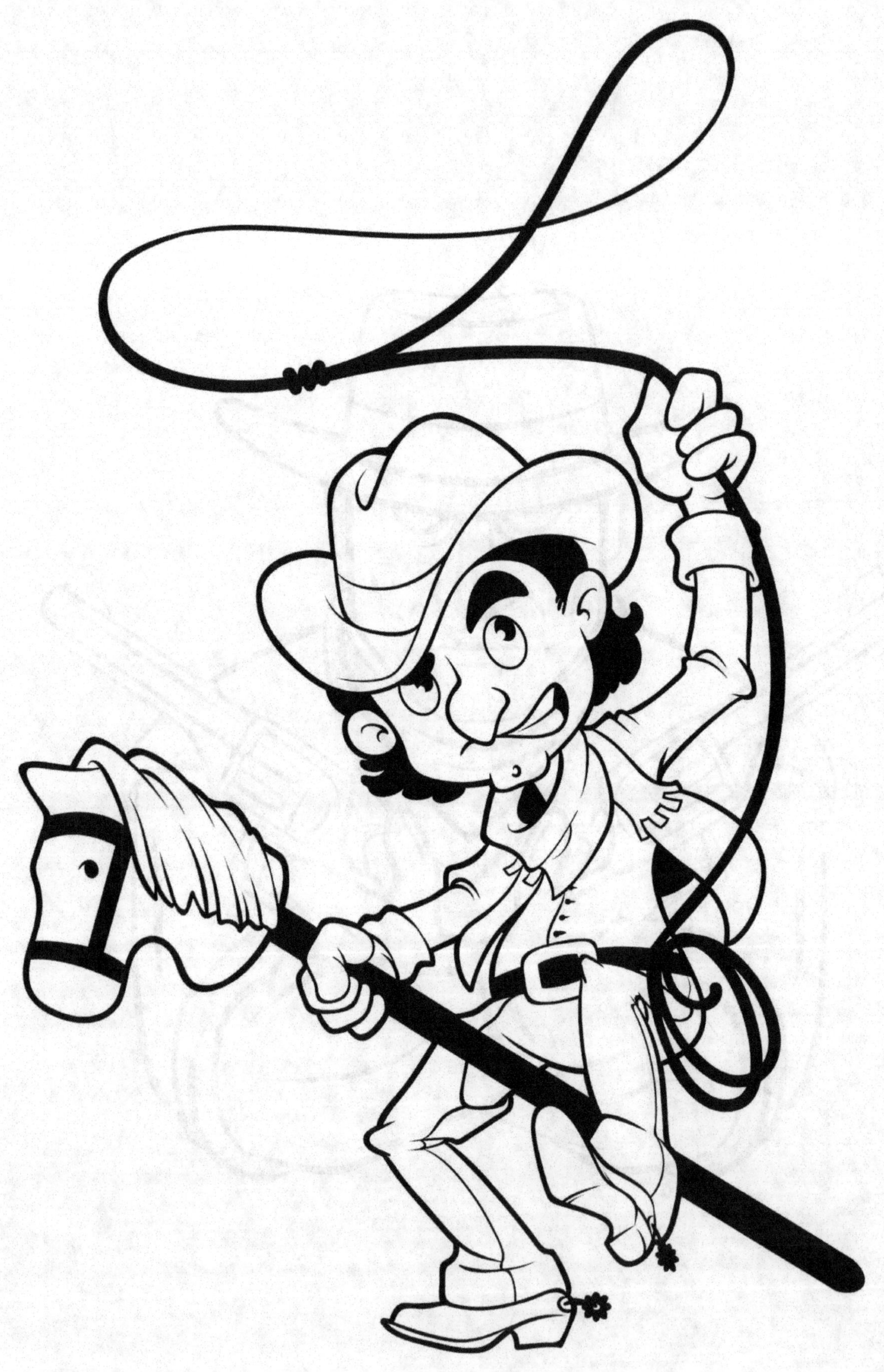

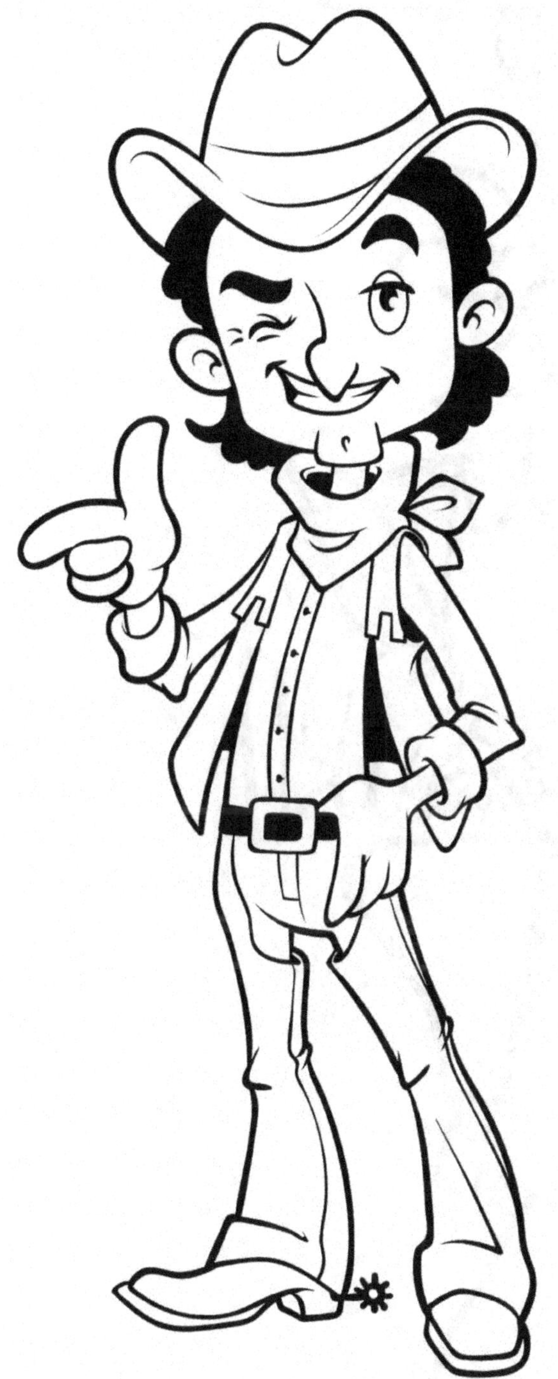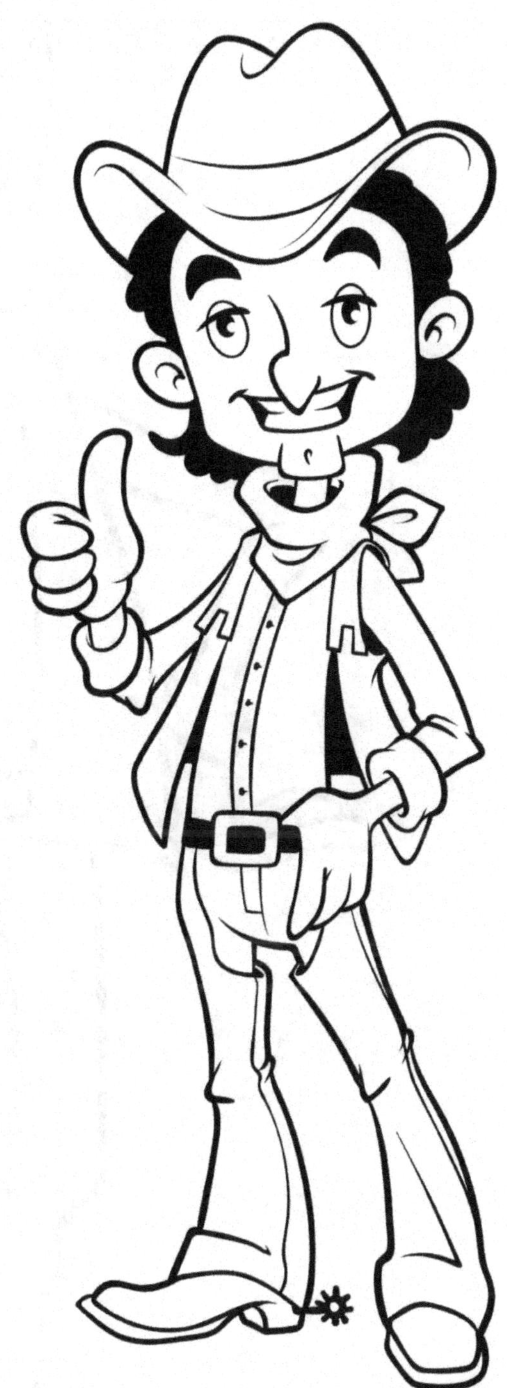

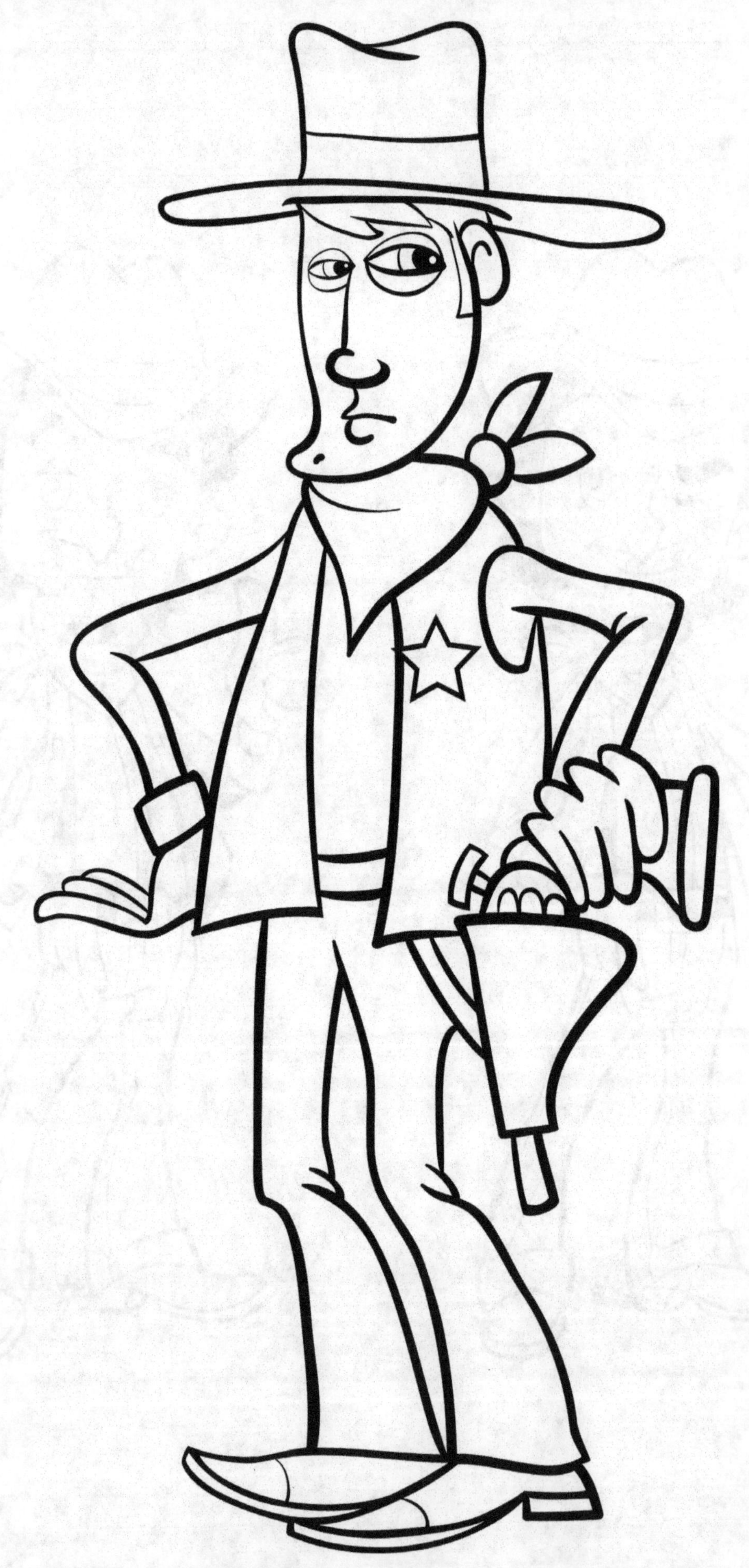

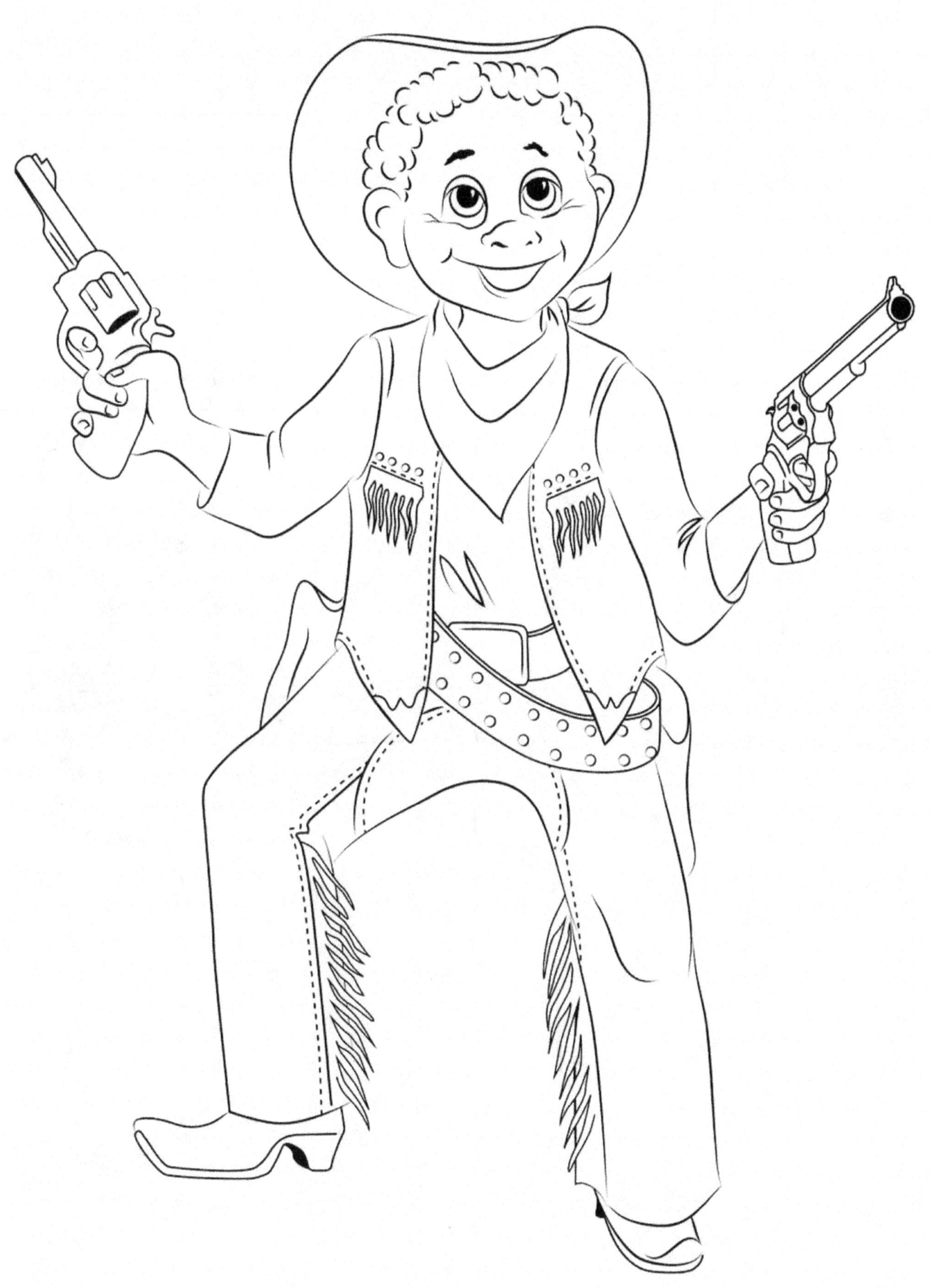

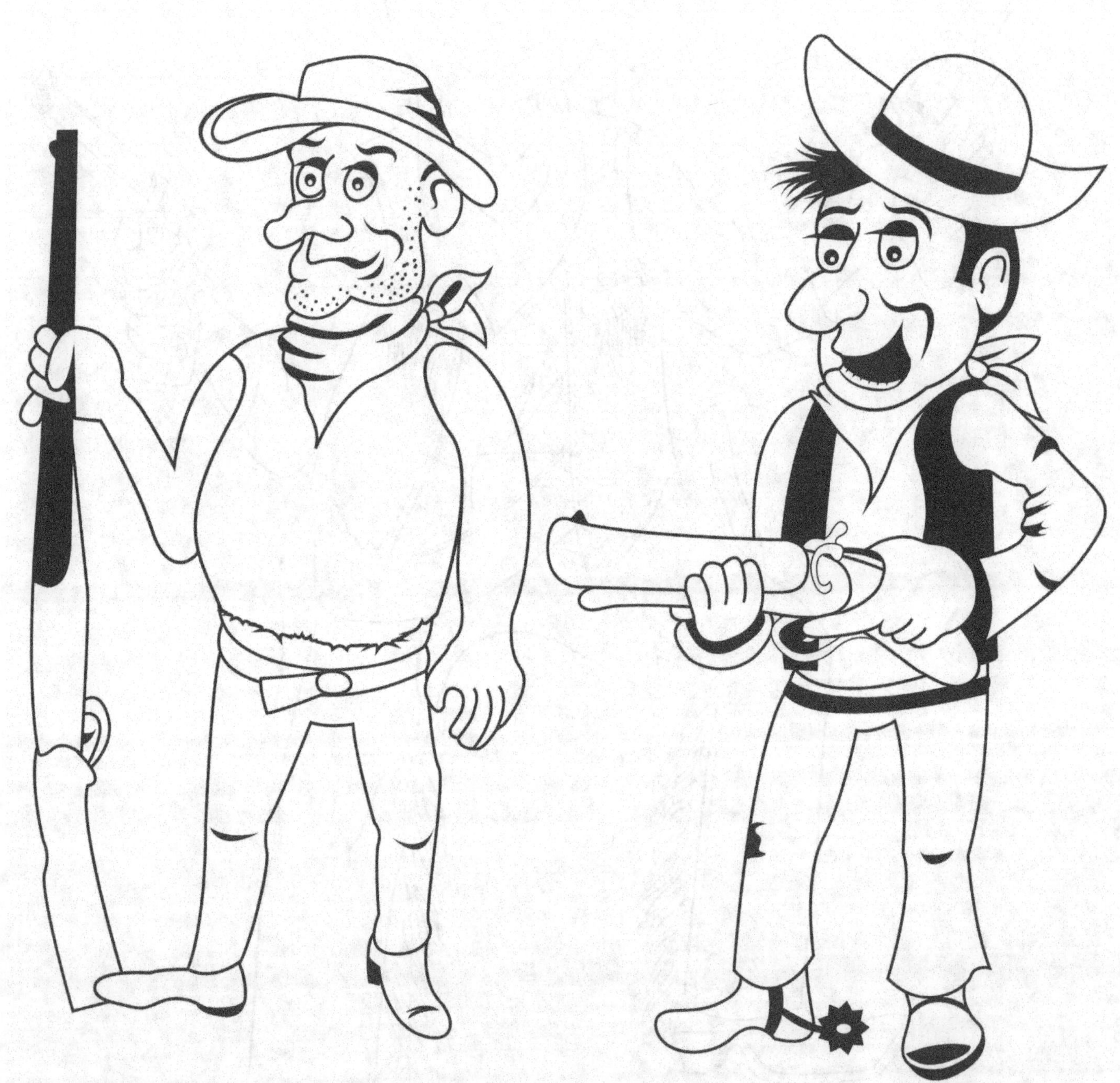

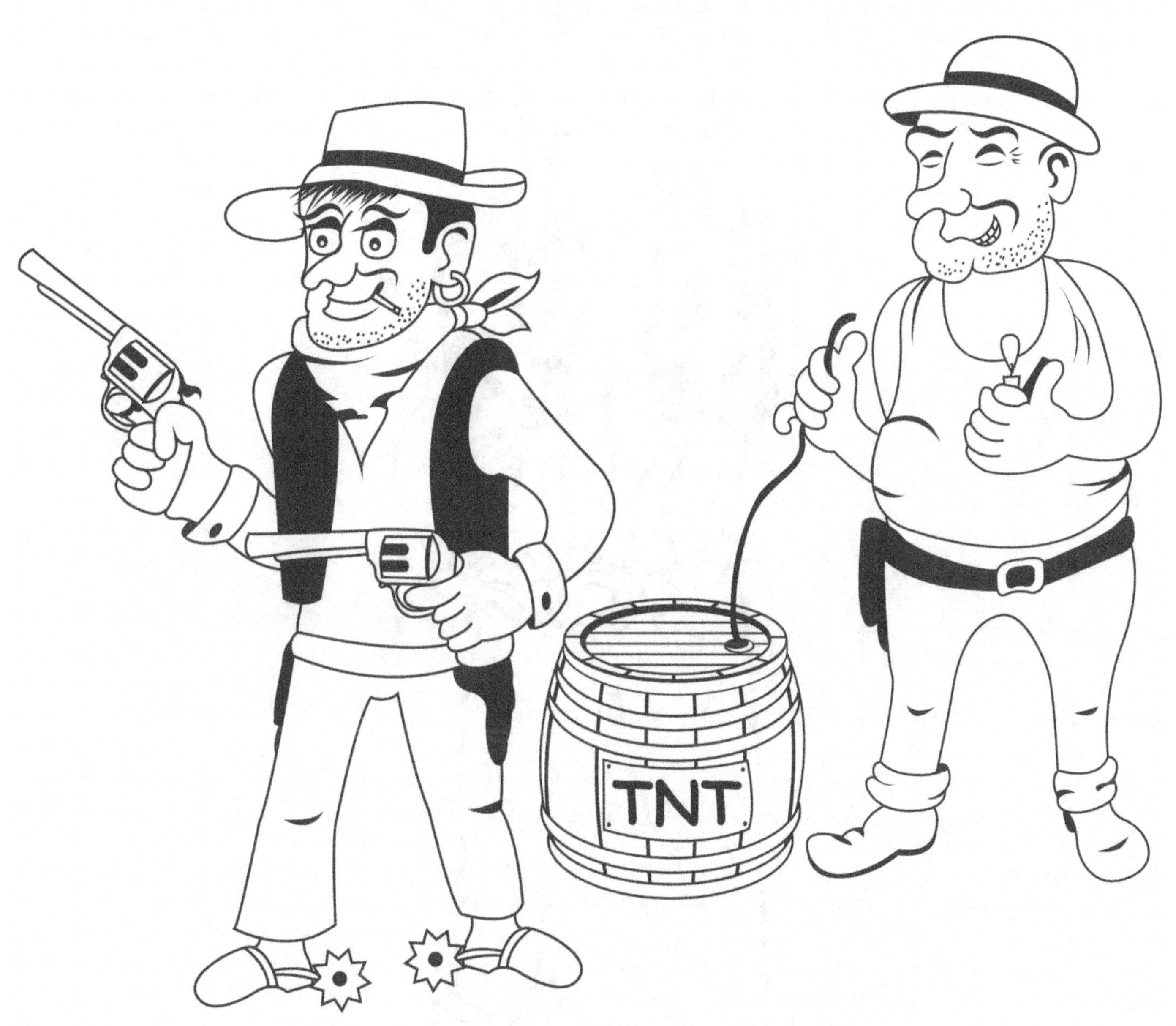

TNT

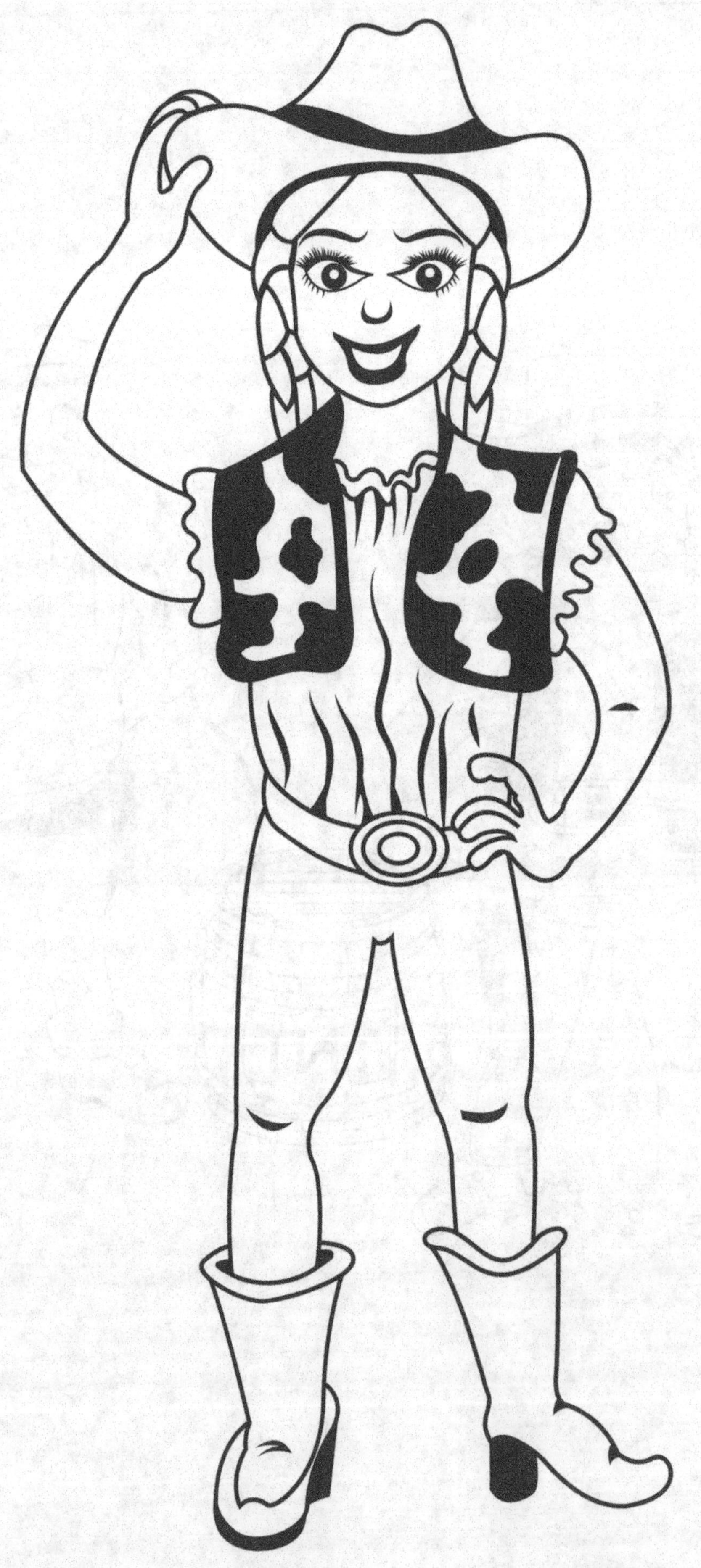

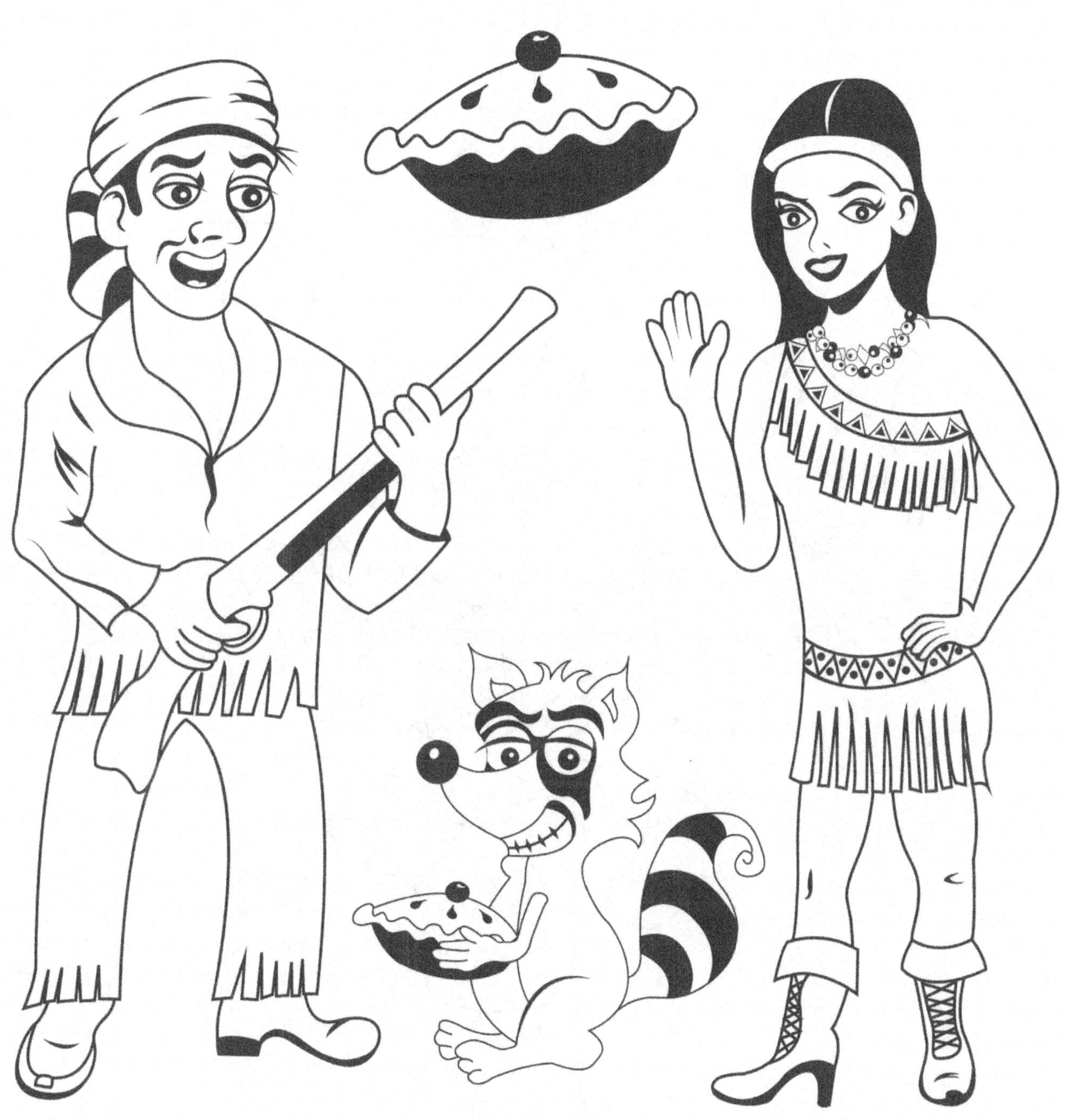

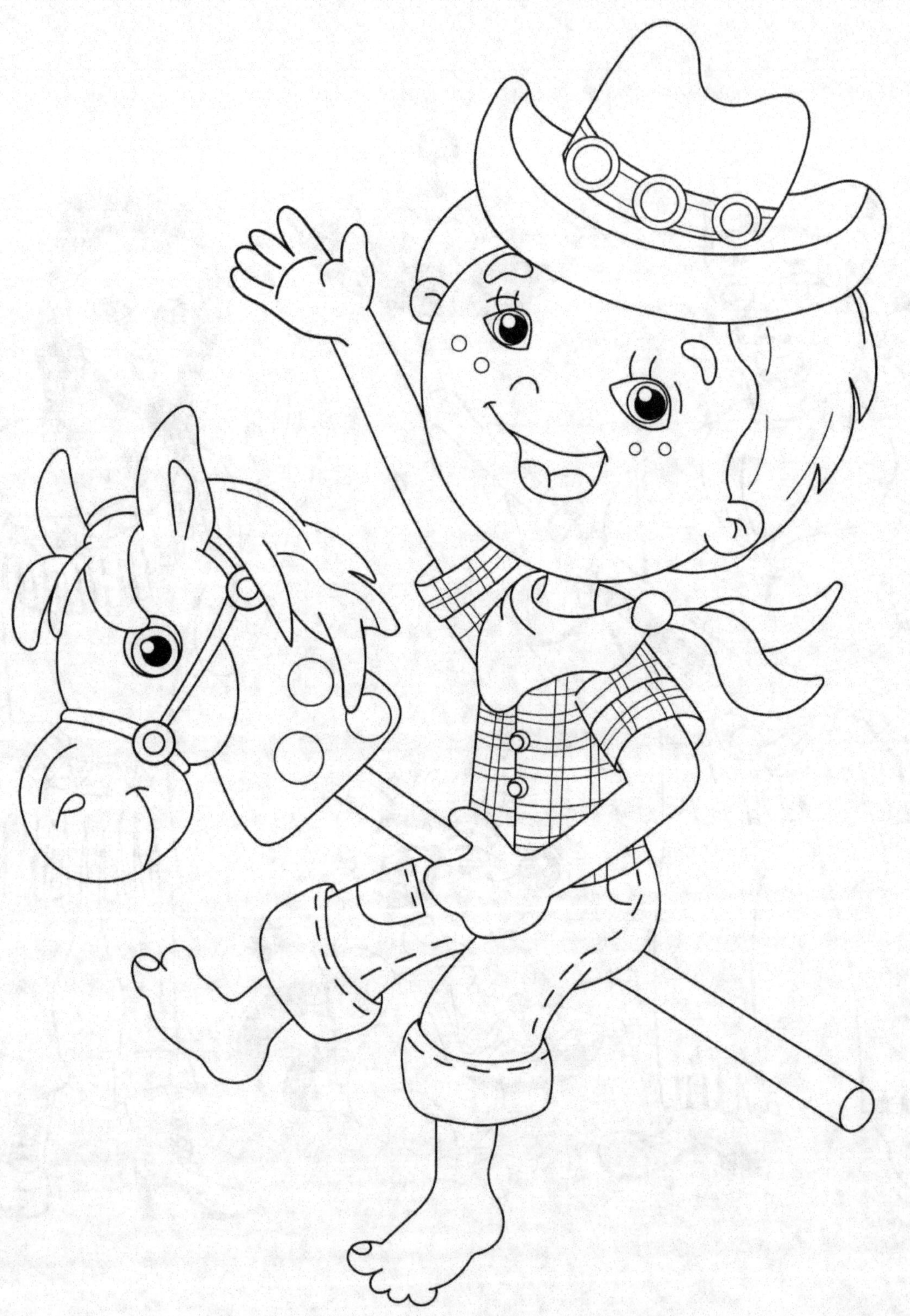

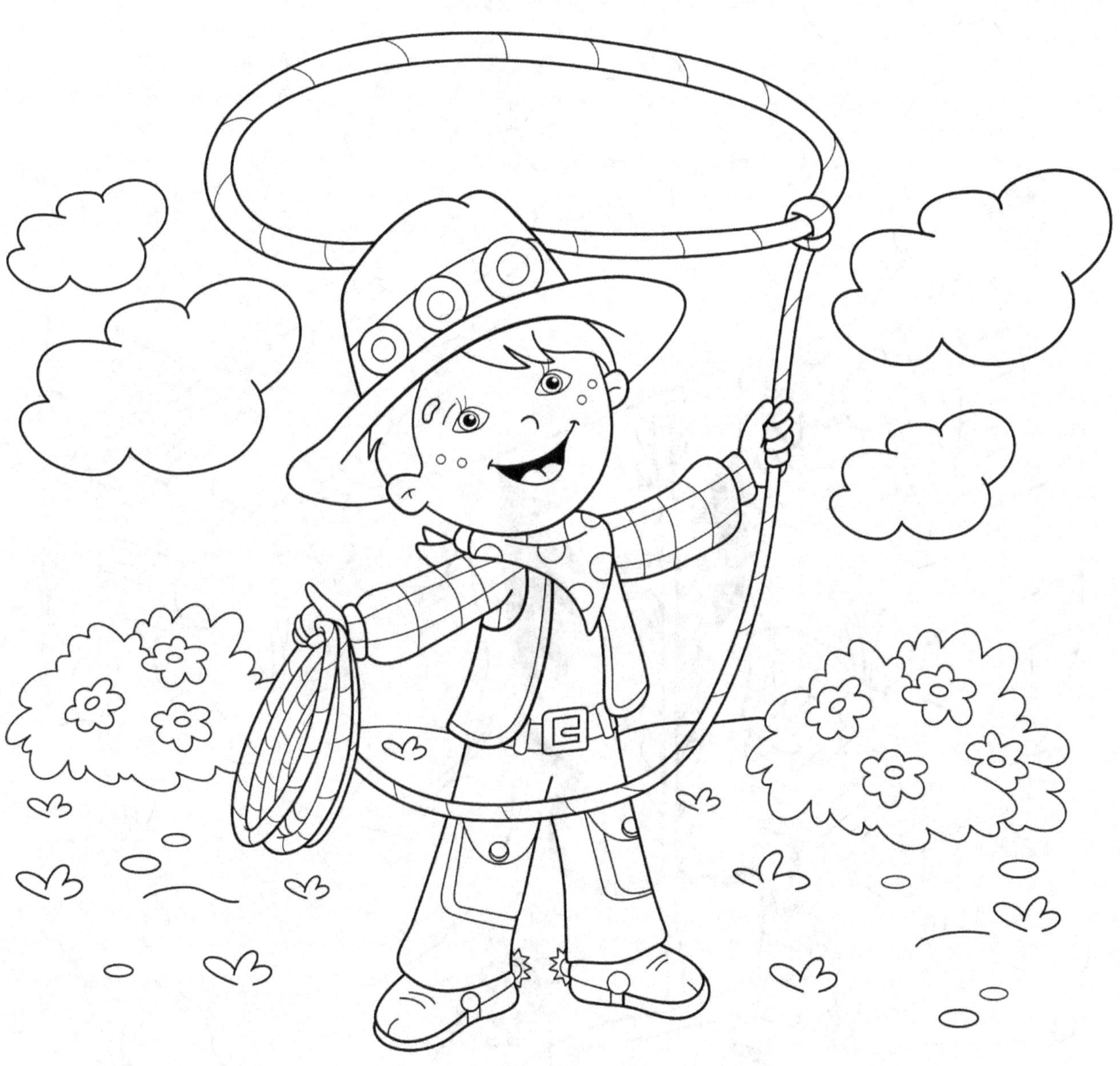

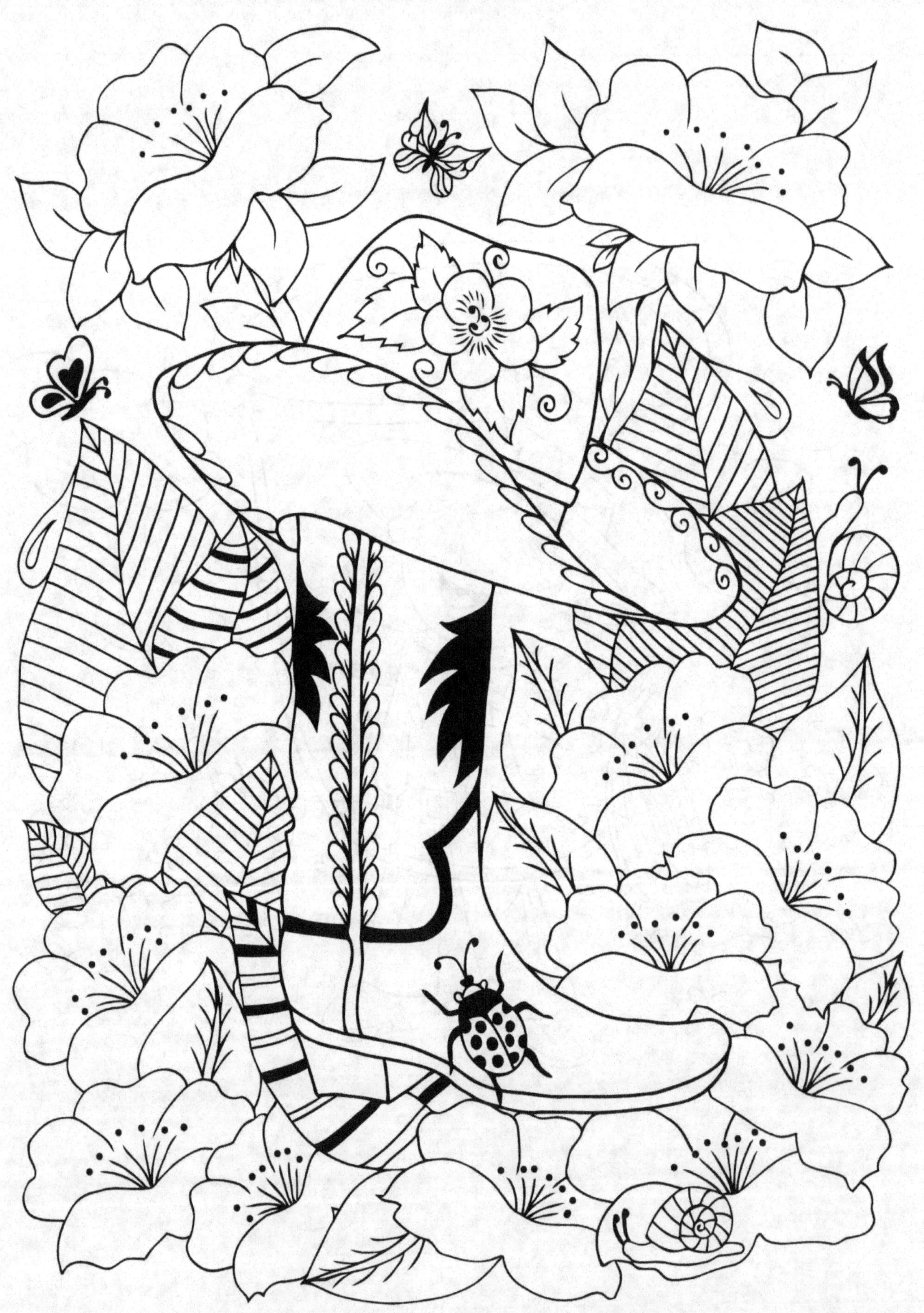

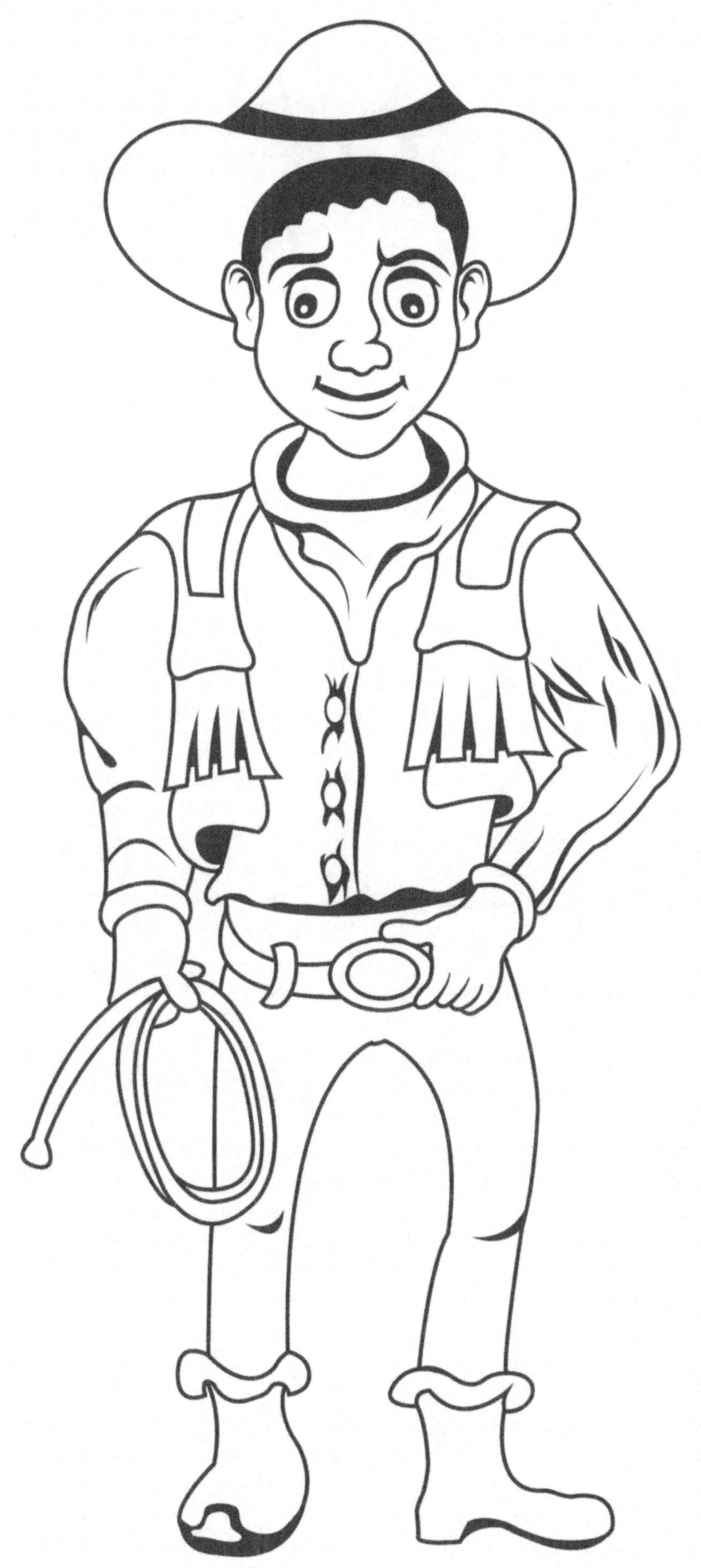

www.ingramcontent.com/pod-product-compliance
Lightning Source LLC
Chambersburg PA
CBHW082243060726
47598CB00016B/2758